ADVICE FROM A STRANGER

Olivia Mulligan

Fisher King Publishing

ADVICE FROM A STRANGER

ISBN 978-1-914560-03-3

Fisher King Publishing
The Old Barn
York Road
Thirsk
YO7 3AD
England
www.fisherkingpublishing.co.uk

For my Dad

If 'Alright' means inspiring, brave and one-of-a-kind, then yes, I guess you're 'Alright.'

"Olivia must keep writing! She has talent, wit and insight and it's a joy to read."

- Georgey Spanswick, BBC Radio York

"We all have moments when we feel like we are at a cross roads. Asking a stranger for directions saves us from getting lost. The life lessons shared through poetry inspired by strangers in this wonderful book will do just that - guide you on your journey through life!"

- Niri Patel – MD of fit20 & Executive Director BNI Yorkshire

"A new national treasure has emerged!"

- Rich Hayden – MD of Sevensun

"Superb poetry and what a great idea behind the book."

- Keith Madeley MBE

"Olivia Mulligan administers her second dose of pandemic-era poetry, responding to the advice of seventy strangers with seventy poems shot through with enlivening optimism, humour and invention. Weaving together the bizarre, the beautiful and the banal, these poems are a shot in the arm that'll make you feel the world's that little bit brighter than you thought."

- Antony Dunn, Poet

"I adore this book. It's funny, witty, it made me laugh and it stopped me in my tracks."
- Emma-Jane Hinds, Actor & Writer

"Fantastic concept, amazing poetry!"
- Alan Reynolds – Author of Flying With Kites

"If you want my advice - read this book."
- Andy Croft, Ripon Poetry Festival

"It's alright."
- Tom Mulligan, Olivia's Father

I asked 70 **strangers**,
"Please give me a piece of life advice."

I used their responses as inspiration
to write my next poem.

This poetry collection is the result.

Waiting

We miss our train to indulge in waiting
staring at commuters – modern life hating
data roaming is dominating
queues in the crowds complicating
overcrowded bodies decorating the station where we
have missed our train.

Why does this always happen? This painful waiting
welcoming whizzing thoughts in heads creating
critical nonsense & tight chests dictating
irregular
heartbeats and inner dialogue
debating
- Why me?

We miss our train to indulge in waiting
but amongst the chaos and modern life hating
we see a Stranger's Smile illuminating -
of course we smile back, without hesitating.
Smiling
to the Stranger
who has also missed their train.

Life advice from Josh Peaty
Everything happens for a reason

White Knuckles

Doctor, Doctor,
This isn't a joke
But I cannot stand
That nasty bloke.
Of course I can stand
I have legs and feet –
But he has a face
That I'd like to beat –
Beat up with my fists,
My knuckles white –
I'd rather be blind
Than have him in sight.
For the sight of him
My blood will boil
My teeth will clench
My spine recoil...
Doctor, Doctor
I beg you to help –
Help me hurt him
Make him yelp –
Make him suffer
And then disappear –
Or make him stay
But live in fear.

The Doctor stared
Studied my sickness...
Then prescribed a potion
Named 'Forgiveness.'
She crossed out 'twice'
To take three times daily

Take with food,
Boldly and bravely.

Life advice from Jodie
Forgive and forget

Happy Days

Don't worry,
Be Happy
Happily listening to Bob Marley
Hardly worrying at all

Repeat.

Don't worry,
Be Happy
Happily listening to Bob Marley
Hardly worrying at all

Repeat.

Don't worry,
Be Happy
Happily listening to Bob Marley
Hardly worrying at all

Shuffle

Cos every little thing - is gonna be alright
Yes Bob. Yes it is.

Shuffle

Pause

Play

Play
I said, Play

Play!

Why isn't it working?

Life advice from Bob Deamer
Be happy

Help Your Mother

"Why haven't you helped your Mother today?
She's been doing housework like a looney."
"I've been volunteering at the Nursing Home, Dad
So my CV looks good for uni."
"You ungrateful sack of potatoes
Gallivanting with old folk all day
Leaving your Mother to peel the potatoes
Young lass, what have you got to say?"
"Dad. They've got dementia.
They really appreciate my visits."
"What good is university?
If your roast dinners aren't exquisite?"
"Dad. There's more to life than Yorkshire puddings."
"Young lass. You take that back.
Chores must be done. Respect must be paid.
Volunteering is for maniacs!
That's why I don't help your Mother
I'm not voluntarily wasting my time
Besides. She likes to feel useful.
So I'm actually being kind."
"I'm not quite sure it works like –"
"Lass. What've I said about respect?
I'm sat here nicely. Watching the footie.
Respectfully not getting wrecked."

Life advice from William Bell
Be nice and kind to everybody

The Ultimate Con

being an adult is a fusion –
the fusion of con and
sense that is none
sensing a nonsensical confusion
sensing laundry detergent &
investing in a smart meter

feet are bigger
for bigger shoes
& underwear is sexier
sometimes
(but maybe not)
no – not today –
today I've got a headache

aching heads
heading towards another day
another day
of office screens
and inner screams,
tantrums
tantrumming held tongues
in work-wear suits
suitably, appropriately, respectfully saying
excuse me...

you do know that **tantrumming**
isn't a real word?
you sound absurd
(but that's ok)
being an adult
(isn't real either)

Life advice from Adele Mortimer

Being an adult is a con

Hang On a Sec

it must be positive
if it's not negative
it must be positive
if it's not negative
it must be positive
if
it's
not
negative
on the battery of the broken
dining room clock
mocking time

timely,
at a timely time,
the clock stopped
(so the world stopped)
asking us to take a

moment

to be

Positive

Life advice from Steve Marlowe
Just be positive

Depression Is Like A Landscape

the arty trees
like arteries
or veins
from the ground

grounding the sound
of a winter heart -
beating
to a halt

for a moment -
you're not there -
to stare -
at the trees -

the arty trees
like arteries
or veins
from the ground

grounding the sound
of a growing heart
capturing
a breath of Spring

Life advice from Amanda Lennon
Everything passes

Said With a Grin or a Gin or Both

Perhaps when I'm 40 I will be less naughty
but then again probably not.
I'll have more money and it will be funny
to spend all my dollar on pot.
Oh dear you're choking.
Gosh I was joking.
For a druggy I am certainly not.
I'm certainly free from artificial glee
I've just naturally lost the plot.

Perhaps when retired, I won't get fired
But then again probably not.
With husband number three, it must be me
I just enjoy tying the knot.

Perhaps when I'm grey, I'll be less astray
But then again probably not.
For my hair will be pink, I'll still flaunt a wink
With laughter lines that are smoking hot.

Perhaps when I'm dead, I'll regret what I said
But then again probably not.

Life advice from Julie
Just enjoy it

Grandad Morris

sometimes
sandcastles are swept away
collapsing the precious
grains
of
sand –
needing,
needing,
needing a helping hand

The boats are made of wood
But the men are made of steel
whispered Grandad Morris
from a knowing land
knowing,
knowing,
knowing she would rebuild her castle

sometimes
sandcastles are swept away
collapsing the precious
grains
of
sand –

ready
to start again

Life advice from Tamara
From trauma comes opportunity

Wrong Again

I ask my Brain -
the box in the skull - tell me now.
Is it push or pull?
(Brain always gets it wrong)

I ask my Gut -
my inner studio - tell me now.
Which way do I go?
(Gut always gets it wrong)

I ask my Soul
(my Gut's Yogi Master) - tell me now.
Tell me what to do.
(Soul doesn't respond)

I ask again -
this time say please. Please tell me now
Please tell me what to do.
(Soul still doesn't respond)

Brain pipes up -
Speaking once more - I'll tell you how -
I can help you -
I can help you open the door.

I give a forceful push –
amongst life's rush - cheekbones flush
with embarrassed defeat
(it was a pull).

I ask my Brain –

I ask again –
Why –
Why –
I always get it wrong

Life advice from Georgia Roberts

You're asking the wrong person

The Colour Under The Blue

I dreamt that I was dreaming in a dream
A world where footsteps wandered with the rain
A daydream day that delicately seems
To wander without fear through harsh terrain

I slept the sort of sleep I never knew
Unable to arise to blackbird chimes
Instead my chest drowned deep into the blue
Singing with the ocean's heavenly rhymes

I whispered to the waves under my breath
A cosy chill caressed my sleeping spine
Floating free from the frozen icy death
I'm diving to the place my eyes can shine

I'll sparkle amongst coral reefs that seem
Too bright to see unless you're in my dream

Life advice from Jake Houghton
Follow your dreams

Pause

her boots were glamorously dressed
deep in mud from last night's rain
from where she paused in wild wind -
panoramic views began to explain;

sequins fell from the sky
dreadlocking her hair, her mane,
she listened to the vastness, the open hills
climbing on her paused terrain;

climbing to a certain stillness
forgetting the exterior rain
realising her beauty, her truest smile
smiling - she needn't explain;

Life advice from Eileen
Press the pause button. Look, listen and enjoy

New Times Roman (Bold)

I will not blame him - the man with the ink
Tattooing my chest after several drinks
Perhaps I'll reminisce and I'll think
'That was a mistake.'

Nope. Not me. No mistakes here
Mistakes may happen but they disappear
Unlike permanent ink, bold and clear:
Clearly reading, 'No Regrits'

Life advice from Jasmine
Have no regrets

Running Is All That I Know

A Coach once told me I was 'good'
A Coach once told me that I should
'Push myself to see my true potential.'

A Coach once told me to eat more rice
A Coach once told me to bathe in ice
A Coach once told me to try a little harder.

A Coach once told me I could make the trials
A Coach once told me to run more miles and
'Get used to feeling uncomfortable.'

A Coach once told me to embrace the pain
A Coach once told me to do the lap again
A Coach once told me to stop crying.

A Coach once told me 'no more wine'
A Coach once told me to 'watch the waist line'
And no, that's not a film.

A friend once told me that I was 'good'
A friend once told me that I should
'Do the right thing - and take a day off.'

Life advice from A Tired Runner:
(He didn't seem too chirpy so I didn't go as far as asking his
name. He looked like a Daniel)
Don't run too fast on a Saturday morning

Intentionally Lost

Winding pavements wiggled a longer route
Life was waiting, expecting my return
As I crunched through the autumn fallen fruits
Feeding my steps with frost and orange burn

Turning, touching moss on an untouched gate
Opening a stillness for busy eyes
I'm wisely lost with slow steps to be late
Later feasting on sweet October skies

The mainstream clouds are somewhere else today
They're following a trendy southern breeze
But here, for now, with this sky, I will stay
I stare, I listen, alone, I'm at ease

Now, in June, I'm on a different trail
Intentionally lost to write my tale

Life advice from Ben
Always take a different path

Kind Of A Little Kind Poem

kindly imagine a little more kindness
being a little kinder each day
each day all kinds of kind gestures
gesturing kind thoughts to say
kind words –
kindly imagine a kinder world
the kind where different kinds of names
all kindly tried to be kinder
all kinds would kind of feel the same

Life advice from Joanne
(the kind lady on the phone as I renewed my car insurance)
Always be kind to people

Stare At The Stars

Yesterday's
Cuban cigars
Expensive cars
Electric guitars
Exclusive bars
To hide the scars
Of yesterday
When yesterday
Was yesterday
After yesterday

But in a moment
It will be another
Moment

And this moment
Is asking you
To look up...

And stare...

At the stars...

Life advice from Paul
*We all make mistakes, learn from them and move
forward*

Career Goals

I'm going to be a Doctor
(a Lawyer is my second choice)
My Nan thinks I'd be good at Politics
To be 'The People's Voice.'
But I'm going to be a Doctor
I'll be a Pilot on the side
When Dad tells folk I'm studying medicine
It fills him with Fatherly pride.
He didn't mind the little white lie
He thought my career goals were fantastic
Too young for college at 4 years old
My hospital was plastic.
At the wise old age of ten
I broke some painful news
I didn't want to be a Doctor
I realised I wanted to choose...
My Teacher spoke of possibilities
Perhaps the Army with all the gear?
I could work 'in Sport' or 'in Fashion'
Or I could be an Engineer?
At 16 my Uncle told me
An 'Accountant' would be stable
A side effect might be depression
But I'd have comfort that I'm able– to afford a nice suit.
Money seemed to be important
I wanted to earn more than my sister –
So my teenage self wouldn't believe that
My dream job would be a Barista.
"So is it true you just make coffee?"
(The 'just' is emphasised).
I JUST make the 'best' coffee

And my life isn't compromised –
But life is enhanced as their taste buds dance
As they sip the artist's work
Guzzling the knowledge of farming, roasting,
As I peacefully watch, I smirk
I smile daily as I witness
Daily happiness each day
Yet each day I will witness heart break
I'll see loneliness and I'll say – this one is on us.
So no, I don't JUST make coffee
I don't just pour, froth and swirl
I study laughter, blushing and silence
I learn what makes the world.

Life advice from Helen Vaux
Don't follow the crowd. It's fine to carve your own path

Beginning To Believe

Praised for my long eye lashes
by The Eyelash Talent Scout
who wasn't a scout but a man on the bus
(also not afraid to shout)
SHAME ABOUT THE REST OF YA FACE

Bus man didn't approve of my face like face
But he thought my long eyelashes were 'great.'
Were all long things desirable?
Alas, no. Some long things we 'should hate.'

Praised for my long eyelashes
by a girl in the year above
who also mocked my long nose hairs
and said I'd never fall in love.

Praised for my long eyelashes
by friends and strangers too.
A long nose, however, is not desirable
Mum asked what I was going to do -
plastic surgery?

Praised for my long eyelashes
saving money on eyelash extensions.
It seems I'm only good for my long eyelashes
my desirable eye hair dimensions.

I once stood tweezering my nose hairs
imagining bald eyelashes too.
Who decided which hairs to praise?
what 'ideals' we should pursue?

My eye lashes are quite big headed
my nose hairs are quite depressed.
But still I tweezer my sad nose hairs
forever trying to impress –

Life advice from Stephen Wilkinson
If you throw enough crap at the wall, some of it will stick

I Can't Hear You

Pardon? I can't hear you
My ears are clogged up
Bogged down
With yesterday's paperwork
Working out tomorrow's
6 o'clock news headlines &
Underlining next week's
<u>Big Weekly Shop</u>

Stop.
Say again?
I missed that message -
Too busy
Messaging
With indented thumbs.

Could you repeat that?
Actually
Not now -
Don't repeat that
Not now -
I don't have time
Not now -

I might
Maybe
Have time to listen
Later
But if I don't have time
For Nigel Slater's
Quick & Easy Midweek Suppers

I won't have time
To listen
To you.

Who? Listen to who?

I asked the muffled distant voice
(the one whispering what to do) –
Tell me who you are? I said
The voice replied, *I'm You.*

Listen...

Life advice from Anya Harris
Listen to your inner tuition

I Must Write

I can't pick and choose when the poems come
But I must, there and then, write them down
So I'm sorry you've fallen in the canal
And I'm sorry you're about to drown

Just doggy paddle a few more minutes?
The next verse I've got is gold
Just keep calm – the water won't kill you
You'll probably die from the cold

No I'm not 'just watching' – I'm thinking –
About the metaphor of an icy heart
The mystical mist and then a poetic twist
Seductive syllables soon start

Right. Enough of your amateur dramatics.
Come here. Get out. I'll save you.
What a waste of time, the poem barely rhymed
I need something more for my debut...

Hey! What the hell are you doing?
Sopping wet and down on one knee?
What's that in the box? That diamond rock?
"Olivia, will you marry me?"

Hang on a sec, that reminds me
Of those lyrics I dreamt last night
I'll get back to you in a moment dear
But before I answer, let me write.

Life advice from Phillip Wilby
Write it down

Revelations of Divine Love

In darkness we hear music
Mimicking charms of holy bells
Ringing silver toned stories
Of smoky shadows that might tell
Stories of future twilight
Tales that sunrise soon will swell
Love will be lost (only to be found)
Finding melody in each gloomy cell
Each darkness offers music
Sung by our Mother Earth's carousel
"All shall be well and all shall be well
and all manner of thing shall be well."

Life advice from Wendy Wilby
*As said by Mother Julian: "All shall be well and all shall
be well and all manner of thing shall be well"*

Listen, Child

I like to think
Daydream
One day I'll have children
One day I'll procreate
I'll gain weight
And I'll Facebook update that I'm a Mum

I like to think
Daydream
One day I'll have children
I'll have children that will love me
After the midwife has shoved me
With gas and air and hey presto
Bob's your Aunty
A small human will love me until the end

I like to think
Daydream
One day I'll have children
I'll have the privilege to say
You should wear a vest, it's November,
I'll spot their bare skin on display
They'll groan and grunt like I've ruined their day
Wearing some ghastly crop top.

I like to think
Daydream
That one day I'll have children
My children will learn from own red flags
My children will learn from my niggly nags
My children will learn life's greatest lesson:

Do
Not
(I repeat, do not)
Do Not
Buy
The
Cheap
Bin bags.

Life advice from Jade Wright
Never buy cheap bin bags

The Night I Smashed My iPhone Screen And Shared a Taxi With a Man Called Enrique Inglesias Who Wasn't Actually Enrique Inglesias

burgundy grape juice
to line the stomach
getting lucky
finding a fiver
fizzy poison to do an all nighter.

brighter
sequins and sparkles –
aero blue
acid green
blush pink
vomit next to the sink, sat there
dance on.

dance with dandelion yellow
disco pants.

Life advice from Nev Atkinson
Don't mix your drinks

The Fall

our language turns to ice

skating a whispered dance

dancing a silent love song

gliding off the mountain tops

falling into unknown air

knowing we will be saved

Life advice from Becky Goddard-Hill
Trust in love

Sleep On It

I explained my stress like a sticky mess
A lagoon of hot rods and fire
Burning blisters on blistered flesh
A carpet of knives and barbed wire.

I said, *"a carpet of knives and barbed wire."*

The therapist blinked and then he inked
A scribble with his roller ball pen.
'Burning blisters on blistered flesh'
I continued to voice once again.

The therapist recommended meditation
Followed by a good night's sleep.
I'm sure if he slept on barbed wire
His slumber would not be too deep.

For fifty pounds an hour
(Which includes the pandemic discount)
He prescribed taking a walk
And suggested I breathe in and out.

I'm not sure I want to 'sleep on it'
I'd rather sleep away...
Away from the stress and the sticky mess
And without fifty quid to pay.

I guess that includes my glass of water
And half a box of Kleenex
And the comfort that someone will listen
And that crying is a natural reflex.

Finally he hinted I take a shower
(i.e. suggesting that I reek)
I left the session feeling worse than before
But still I said, "see you next week."

Life advice from Jane Dean
Sleep on it

To Titivate

(Verb): *To Make Minor Enhancements To*

The mischief making
of participating
stimulating
illustrating
a possible world

articulating
reciprocating
originating new ideas
titivating your previous world.

Don't await
to titivate
to renovate
the mileage rate
at which your world expands

to titivate
will elevate
then innovate
recreate
a new world in your hands

Life advice from Catherine Cooper
There is always time to read

Give & Take

Take the cake
Give them a slice
Take a break
Pay the price

Take up space
Give up your seat
Accept the coffee
When you hear 'my treat'

Take the compliment
Give kind words
Listen to others
Make your voice heard

Take each morning
Give a stranger a chance
Take their experience
Let the world dance

Take each sunrise
Give time for the storm
Take each moment
The memories will form

Life advice from Ann
It's all about give and take

The Master Key

Me old man always said
Try 'ard at school – don't end up like me
And his old man always said
Try 'ard at school – that could be your master key.

Then I'll spend eighteen years
Telling my son the same
But my son thinks he knows better
He will continue the mischief game.

Spending eighteen years telling *his* son
Don't end up like me
Try 'ard at school and see the world
That could be your master key...

Life advice from Ian Hussey
Pay attention to the teacher so you don't have to spend
all day groveling around on the floor

A Love Letter To The Hurt

To the green gummy bear,
To the Bounty,
To the phlegm,
To all the moist and crusty words,
Never used again.

To one ply toilet paper
To anchovies,
To clowns,

To Luton,
To Scunthorpe
& all bullied towns

To text messages fails –
'failure sending,'
To published books –
With terrible endings

To pistachios that don't open,
To the trains that are late,
I'm sorry for the lack of love,
I'm sorry for the hate.

Life advice from Ken Sommerville
Always give people a chance

How Was Your Day?

Udderly ordinary
Perhaps a little wonky
A car did a honky
And said 'show us your melons.'

Cantaloupes I think.

Husband asked again,
So how was your day?
I said OK
Because I think melons are better than mosquito bites.

He asked what did I mean
And I said I'd seen
My friend Olivia who has mosquito bites
Inherited from her Mum's bee stings.

He didn't understand
Instead he reached out his hand
To confirm I had
Cantaloupes -
Fried eggs.
Yorkshire puddings.
Baps.
The twins'.
Ant & Dec .
Snuggle pups.
Cat flaps.

Life advice from Laura Quigley
Keep your chin up. Otherwise you're looking at your boobs all day

Sydney

Sydney.
Syd.
You did everything a dog should
& everything
a dog shouldn't
& we couldn't
have loved you more.

Syd.
Thank you.
Thank you for the laughs
the love
the licks.
Thank you
for being you
with your endless list of tricks.

Beg. High five. Speak. Roll over.
Leopard crawling across the floor.
BANG (Dad shot you), playing dead,
& then you'd be back for more.

"Sing us a song," Dad would say.
You would howl a tune we know.
You would follow our every word.
You would wait hours until we said:
'Go' –

Ok Syd!
Siddy it's OK.
Wait.

Now off you go.
Here Syd.
Come here Syd!
I love you more than you know.

My little man
of black, white and tan,
my brother since aged eleven.
Sweet dreams my old boy.
Fetch that toy.
But first, wait - for me, in heaven.

Syd Mulligan (21.02.05 - 12.01.21)

Life advice from Adelia Hallet
Love hard

That's Nice

Being nice is being nice
It's nice to be nice
Because it feels nice
To be friendly
Kind
Lovely
Good –
Delightful
Fine
Charming & we should
All be nice.

We should all be
Peachy
Inviting
Pleasant
Polite –
We should be swell
Fine & dandy
Helpful
And then we might
Have a nicer life.

But what is this 'nice?'
What does it mean?
Is niceness inherited?
Or is niceness seen?

It's warm cookies
Pink sunsets
Glow worms

Fresh mint –

Cherry blossom
Silent cliff tops
Having to squint –
At the dazzling morning light.

Stained glass windows
Handwritten love notes –
It's Yorkshire tea
It's buttery toast.

It's homegrown tomatoes
It's the smell of fresh bread –
It's memories of the ocean
And when the ocean said: listen.

It's unexpected smiles
It's winter spice –
It's truly believing
That's nice, that's nice.

Life advice from Adam Skipper
*Surround yourself with nice people and you'll have a nice
life*

Meaningless Seventeen

disappointment comes
when the words of a haiku
have little meaning

Life advice from Louisa Walters

No expectations, no disappointments

'Sue' Smith

My treehouse in Jakarta
Was built by Mrs Carter's secret lover
Called Sue.

You wouldn't have thought a treehouse so tall
Could be built by someone as small
As Sue.

It's true. But what's false is her name –
You, see, it was all a game, and Sue was actually called
Philomena Smith.

Timid and quiet Philomena
So small that no one had seen her.
Became Sue.

Philomena-now-Sue, she knew what to do
She would grow and she would show the world
Knowledge.

Sue won a Nobel Prize as she studied particles prancing,
Then as a famous physicist, she won Strictly Come
Dancing
And The Great British Bake Off.

Sue was unstoppable but wanted something more
She collected PHD's in German, Art and Law
And Dairy Herd Management.

That still wasn't enough. She needed a passion
Something more than fitness or travel or fashion.

Behold, Extreme Ironing.

It was at the Household Appliance shop, she met Mrs
Carter
They laughed and they loved in their treehouse in Jakarta
Made by Sue.

I sit here now and I read about Sue
I think about my own stories and realise there are few...
But there is always time.

The last page of Philomena's book tells me to go
To go forward and be curious and seek out
What I don't know.

Life advice from Sally Jones
*Make yourself an expert in a couple of areas you really
love*

I'll Have A Glass Of Sparkling Water Please

Woe is me with this half empty
Glass of water
That is still.

At least if the liquid were to spill
(Which it probably will)
I'll have less to clean up.

Woe is me with this half empty
Glass of water
That is still.

I'll soon be thirsty with this Controversy
Chat of half full versus
Half empty.

Woe is me with this half empty
Glass of water
That is still.

Woe is me with this half empty
Glass of water
That's not water at all.

My head starts to spin, for it is actually gin
And I wish it were now
Half full.

Woe is me with this half empty
Very empty
Glass of gin.

Life advice from James Woolveridge

If you leave your glass half empty you will never be disappointed

Magic Treasure

the boy treasured a treasure chest
treasuring salted almond
teardrops that once fell from sad
hazel eyes;

the treasure chest will always be a
treasure chest but the teardrops that it
treasures
will one day be tears of joy

Life advice from Evie Milner (aged 8)
Don't be sad, it won't last forever

Get Kettle On

Yorkshire Man is pronounced
Yorkshiremun
(because he is so sure).
And this Yorkshiremun is certain
There is only one true cure:

Tea.

Or gravy.
Nestlin' in a Yorkshire pud.
Then o'course more Yorkshire tea
(other sorts are just no good).

Then a beer. A proper beer.
When y'mouth makes that gulpin' sound.
Then why not – another beer!
But only if it's not his round.

Then back at home the kettle's on –
It's never too late for a brew.
He don't fancy 'no gossip' tonight
Instead, he'll just silently stew...

Life advice from Katy
It's never too late

The Day I Got The Vaccine

surroundings have been bleak - the minutes contaminated
marinated with a boredom - like decaffeinated

coffee without the buzz
a concert without the crowd

instead a crowd of one - shielding & aggravated
itching to get out & to feel fascinated

feeling a needle is in my arm - I think I've just graduated
the school of shielding becomes a memory -
my certificate states 'vaccinated'

memories of bleak surroundings - the minutes
contaminated
marinated with playful words - like caffeinated dreams

Life advice from Lynley Oram
Say what you have done, not what you are going to do

Please Stab My Deltoid, Kind Lady

Her kindness, which stabs into my arm –
Honoured by thy needle.
Thy vulnerable come;
Thy waiting is done
On lists as we wait to be called.
Give us this day our daily strength
And forgive us our weaknesses,
As we forgive our genetics that tend to mock us.
And lead us not into temptation
(the temptation of a social gathering).
For this is our health,
Our future, our story,
For ever and always.
Amen.

Life advice from Dr Carolyn Ryan
(the lady who gave me my Covid-19 vaccination at 6.15pm on a Sunday)
Be kind

I had already had this advice, 'be kind,' which could either mean;
1. *It is quite a common thing to say*
2. *It is an incredibly important message to remember*

Nameless Neighbours

You know... The tall one
The large one
The 'I'll eat it all one.'
Yeah.
The fat one.
No...The small one
The short one
The face like a wart one.

But what about the slim one?
The thin one
The one with the chin.
The messy one
The sticky one
The one without a bin.

You know... The chunky one.
The hunky one.
The hot but smells funky one.

Oh come on. He's the one with the 'eye.'
The one with the Nan who's just about to...
Die?

No fly.
She's off to Barcelona
Flying far from her neighbours
Because they've got Corona.

You know the one.
The one who likes a tipple...
The one who kissed the postman...
He's got a third nipple.

You know the postman...
The one with the post.
Knocks on your door
When you're trying to host
Asks you to sign
Makes you burn the toast.

Speaking of toast
That lass caught the sun...
Heat stroke last Tuesday when she went for a run.

You know. The one with the teeth.
Says that she's a vegan
Except she eats beef.
Married to What's-his-face
Bald man Keith?
No, that was last year
Her new man's got hair.
Swapped baldy in for luscious locks
Ey. Isn't life unfair?

Poor What's-her-name has had it rough.
Lives at number nine.
You know the one. The quiet one.
Haven't seen her for some time.
Oh yes indeed. The quiet one.
Plays the silent game.
I think we ought to go and visit
I think we should ask her name.

Life advice from Seamus O'Flaherty
Always treat people the way you want to be treated

Sister

galloping
wrestling
sledging at top speed

pausing
stretching
taking time to read

breathing
wondering
wandering just to roam

growing
knowing
with you I'm at home

Life advice from Eve Menezez Cunningham

Wherever you go, there you are

Seriously Playful

I'm about to have a job interview
Time is moving oh-so-slowly
So why does it feel like the right time
To do a roly poly

Why do I have the urge
To run outside in the rain
To catch the droplets with my tongue
To dance like I'm insane

I'll dance out of the city
I'll ride a horse somehow
If not a horse, a cow will do and -
Mr Jenkins will see you now...

The job interview begins
Time is moving oh-so-slowly
Do I – don't I – get off my chair
And do that roly poly...

Life advice from Mitch
Don't take life too seriously

The Full Story

Can we say 'I've finished'
If we didn't truly try?

Can a pie without a pastry bottom
Still be called a pie?

Is contemporary art contemporary art
If we don't leave asking – why?

Is a child experiencing childhood
If they don't believe they can fly?

Is wild camping wild at all
Unless we sleep naked under the sky?

Why don't we admit 'I love you'
When we wave our loved ones goodbye?

Tell me: why do we say 'I'm fine?'
When our heart is asking to cry?

Life advice from Joana Mateus
Finish what you started

This Moment

Once upon a ~~time~~ moment

The man realised his duty

The moment the man stopped

Looking

He realised

He was beauty

Life advice from Surat Singh Chauhan
What you seek in temples and mosques and churches lies inside you. So rather than going out, try going in. Try knowing yourself.

Growing

the seed
the idea
to run
to explore -
to search
to climb
& then run some more –

my fire
my earth
my marathon
my fuel -
my story
my mountain
my ocean
my pool

of possibilities

Life advice from Tom (aged 10)
You can do anything, so try everything

Unavoidable Heart Break

If my heart had peripheral vision
Would it still break?
Or for my own sake
Would it fake
A photo-ready smile
& never truly fall
In love

Life advice from Maureen Collins
*Pessimism becomes a self-fulfilling prophecy; it
reproduces itself by crippling our willingness to act
(Howard Zinn)*

It's The Guy From The Door

I never once dreamed
I would have forty memes
Made about little old me

There's YouTube remixes
For quick chuckle fixes
All captured on CCTV

My shoe lace was stuck
I shouted "oh f - iddlesticks what a pickle"
Then realised – what will be, will be

There's a revolving door
There's me on the floor
Still going around on my knees

I'm still bloomin' there
The people still stare
I'm a landmark for all to see

I never once dreamed
I would have forty memes
Made about little old me

Life advice from Russell Taylor
Don't tie your shoe lace in a revolving door

Open The Door

Tick tock
Knock knock

Who's there?
Sue Clair

I don't know who that is

Tick tock
Knock knock

Who's there?
Hugh Blair

I don't know who that is either

Tick tock
Knock knock

Who's there?
Two bears

That sounds dangerous

Tick tock
Knock knock

Who's there?
Blue square

I don't understand

Tick tock
Knock knock

Who's there?
New air

What's wrong with the air we've got?

Tick tock
Knock knock

Who's there?
Who cares? *Just open the door*

Life advice from Giselle Whiteaker
*There are no bad decisions - every new decision opens
a new door*

I Think Those Were The Days

Remember the good old days?
I don't.
I'm too old to remember
You see, I'm 90 this September

(Or is it August...?)

It doesn't matter when
I'm too old to care
Diabetes hates birthday cake
Plus, no one would be there.

(Well, nobody that I like).

I don't really like anybody
And the ones I liked, are dead
I'm not sure about my husband
I last saw him in the shed

(That was 4 years ago and I never went back to check).

I think it was my husband
Or was it my bit on the side?
Age has turned my mind to mush
Life is slow and simplified –

(And amplified if I remember to wear my hearing aids).

Back ache isn't a myth
False teeth aren't as fun as they look
But now and again I smile and remember

The path in life that I took

(And wow, I've had some laughs).

Life advice from Helen Civil
Don't moan about getting old. You're only old until you're dead. Better old than dead!

The Sunday Marathon

Meditate with the mind
Enter THE ZONE
Prepare for the aches
Brace the bones

Motivate the muscles
Focus on the goal
Feel ready in your body
Feel ready with your soul

Tell yourself YOU LEGEND
Tell yourself YOU GOT DIS
As you stretch to grab –
Those CHEESY WOTSITS

You showcase your tracksuit
Your Lycra display
You're focused. You're ready
For a duvet day

Life advice from Ben Hale
Sometimes it's OK to be in a tracksuit

Not a Nike advert

Imagine a moment
Stronger than before
Imagine a moment
Hungry for more -
We'll race it
We'll chase it
We'll double knot lace it -
We'll stride it
We'll glide it
Victory won't hide it -
Imagine a moment
Where we can push through it
Imagine a moment
Where we can just do it

Life advice from Andrew Bell
It's better to regret something you did, than something you didn't

Eleven

On a scale
of 1   to

10

How bad
is the

Pain?

Life advice from Darryl Baker
Life is tough but so are you

The Show Must Go On

keep going
keep doing
keep being
keep seeing
something

keep breathing
keep dreaming
keep growing
keep showing
keep showing up

show up for him
for her
for them
for you
show up to see
to wait
show up to do
something

show up to show off
to be peaceful
to be loud
show up to dance
show up to cry
unapologetically
proud

still going
still doing

still being
still seeing
something

still breathing
still dreaming
still growing
still knowing
you'll show up

Life advice from Amanda Hemmings
Pick yourself up, dust yourself off and start all over again

Waves With Or Without The Ocean

the sides of our lips
move
upwards
towards the Indian sun

sparks alight our hips
spine
triceps
during the vinyasa flow

synchronised passions bloom &
dip
up
then down

like waves
without the ocean
or with the ocean

diving in
amongst the sea salt
riding the waves
to take you home ...

the sides of our lips
move
upwards
towards the Indian Sun

Life advice from Matt Guest-Smith
Ride the wave, see where it takes you

He Loves Me He Loves Me Not

pluck pluck pluck
pluck a melody of petals

from the sunshine part of the daisy
hazily

thinking of you

Life advice from Sara Wood
Love and be loved

If I Have To Tell You To Stop Swinging On That Chair One More Time You Won't Be Allowed Out At Lunch break

Don't lick the jam off the knife
Don't swing on the plastic chair
Don't run by the swimming pool
Don't be rude to Aunty Claire

Don't get in the car with strangers
And don't steal strangers' cars
Don't steal anything at all
Don't illegally get drunk in bars.

Don't sprinkle drugs on your muesli
Don't do drugs at all
(well this escalated from the plastic chair...)
Still.
Don't do that.
You don't want to risk a fall.

Falling will always be a danger
Fear of falling will always be the hype
But today, we fear a coronavirus
So wash that chair with a santised wipe.

Life advice from Michael May (aged 9)
Be safe

She Wasn't Giving Up

I saw a girl
no older than six
struggle
to open the window
wondering when
she might give up...

"I won't give up," she said
Through her pink Ribena-stained-lips
Wiping back her tufty hair
Styled with dolphin hair grips.

"I won't give up," she said
"I need to show how much I care."
The girl battled with the window
Balancing on a questionable chair.

"I need to say thank you," she said
Because she's been such a friend to me
But kitchens aren't for ladybirds
I need to set her free..."

Life advice from Rithika Raja
Always give back – no matter how small

American Airlines Save $40,000

A lighter load
Through the clouded roads
Of the sky

A tighter mode
Certainly showed
The world – why

Olives are unnecessary.

A lighter load
Through the clouded roads
Of the sky

A tighter mode
Certainly showed
The world – how to save $40,000 each year.

Remove one olive from each passenger's plate
They won't be missed and you'll increase your rate
Of annual income

Life advice from Andy Howe
Don't eat olives, they're awful

This February

last February
we didn't speak
but she was there,

i felt her elbow
softly kiss
my elbow,

winter confetti fell
& the snow settled
nestled on my eyelashes

her eyelashes too
& i said
"we've both got snow on our eyelashes,"

at the time
i didn't clock
my happiness,

but now, February,
without her
i realise She was my precious joy.

Life advice from Nicole Warrior (aged 9):
Spend time with the people you love

Touch

For the first time
In a long time
I pressed the tip of my nose
Against the torso of a tree
Maybe for about nineteen seconds
(I didn't count).
But it was long enough for a bumble bee
To glide a circle around me
And the tree
Anti-clockwise
Three times...
My aunty Kathleen once told me
To not touch the bumble bees
(So I didn't).
But I often wonder
If their stomachs are soft...
I softly remember a time
When I was scared of the bees...
I was the sort of age
When I would wear
Hand-me-down
Dungarees –
Dirty knees
Touching
&
Climbing
The trees –
Every day.

Life advice from Joe Stieger-White
Touch the earth – with your feet, hands, whatever, touch it

I Hope This Email Finds You Well

Dear Sir,
I hope this email finds you well
in your world of publishing, as I await to tell –
share my story with you, from the beginning if I may –
it started with an 'idea' with something to say.
This 'idea' was word chemistry, experimenting with thought –
going off-piste from what I'd been taught...
I know you're very busy so I'll be quick...
But I'd really appreciate your feedback, Rick.
May I call you Rick? I hope you don't mind...
Gosh, look at me babbling. Let's rewind.
Back to the start, to chapter one...
In Tesco car-park - the idea begun.
Usually an Aldi fan, I must confess!
Which do you prefer Rick? (Ah I digress!!)
Excuse my email etiquette, I prefer to write in books!
(Speaking of books. I've written one.) Perhaps you'll take
a look?
I hope I haven't put you off. I hope I haven't blown it.
Many thanks & best wishes,
A rather desperate Poet

Life advice from Tom
If you don't ask, you don't get

Escaping To Be Found

jasmine vines drool petals
melting into hidden
exposed
pristine
dirt roads
of Hong Kong

>this familiar
>lost petal
>in humid air
>in unknown air
>in familiar air
>in alien air
>his air
>her air
>my air
>air that is air
>rare air
>predictable air

>>predicting
>>believing
>>watching
>>the petal breezing past
>>not knowing its past
>>not knowing

>>>it is afraid

Life advice from Jaishree Kumar
Don't put people on a pedestal – they'll fall

She Noticed My Tired Eyes

Like the perfect cup of tea, she carved a moment for me
She didn't ask questions (but she was there)

Her warmth wasn't prickly, her sweetness wasn't sickly
But I needed her (more than I knew)

Pathetic I know, to be feeling so low
About nothing (literally nothing)

She didn't ask why, she just listened to me sigh
Sighing a (lonely) breath

Like the perfect cup of tea, she carved a moment for me
She didn't ask questions (but she was there)

She said it wouldn't fix it, but she offered me a biscuit
and that custard cream **made my day**

I didn't think I'd find it, that moment of kindness,
With a biscuit-carrying stranger on the train

Life advice from Ryan Jackson (aged 8)
Always be kind and considerate to everyone

Bran Means Something To Someone

Do you ever read a poem
& think
What even is that
Pretentious piece of scrap?

I do.

But that pretentious piece of scrap
Yes it might be just that
But it is still
A Poem.

Just like a box of cereal
Is still a box of cereal.

You don't have to like
All of the cereal

(Bran flakes are my favourite).

And I know for a fact
That for many
Bran flakes would be their
'Piece of scrap'
Not worth making.

So if you ever read a poem
& think
What even is that
Pretentious piece of scrap?

That pretentious piece of scrap
Yes it might be that
But it is still
A Poem –

You don't have to like them all.

Life advice from Nicole Robinson
Don't listen to anyone else's advice

The Flavour Of Words

sometimes pomegranate seeds are so red
they taste yellow

& hello moonlight
i am awake

are you asleep?
are you dreaming?

are you dreaming in colour?
acrylic emerald eyes drink vitamin D
tasting the sun's mango nectar

sunshine dances on creased, wrinkled skin
with more lines than a book of stories
sharing memories of younger years
dancing
with sugar -
coated strawberry laces for limbs

are you asleep?
are you dreaming?

keep dreaming

i'll wait until you wake up
so we can continue

this dance

Life advice from Naomi Bonita
Have a vision and walk towards it

The Plain-bellied Emerald

Mountains are like morphine
Flowing rivers of endorphins
Moreishly awakening sleepy veins

Very awake
Very
Very loud silence
Of your heartbeat
Heard
Humming
Humming the melodies
Of a Humming Bird -

The Horned Sungem
        The Blue-throated Hillstar
                Humming through the hills
                    Soaring afar

The Plain-bellied Emerald
        The Bearded Mountaineer
                The Fiery Topaz
                    Flying without fear

Fearlessly

Fearlessly humming with wings

Fearlessly flying
The earth touches feet
Racing to stillness
Can you hear your heart beat

Beating

As time doesn't move
Forwards
Or
Backwards

Up

Or

Down?

Life advice from Owen Simpson (aged 9)
Get outside and do what you love

Catching The Train at 10.49

hey hey
out of my way
can't stop
lungs will pop
head explodes
thoughts erode
I'll be fine
wait in line
wait my turn
my time to learn
to handle unease
to soften the freeze
phone wallet keys
ordering a one way ticket
(please)
replace this time for it's time to embrace
a one way ticket to my
favourite place

Life advice from Jasir (aged 10)
*When you are stressed out, just imagine you are in your
favourite place ever*

10 Words That Rhyme With Run

Training done
Hair in bun
Start line gun
Race begun
Pain is fun?
'G'WARN SON!'
'G'WARN HUN!'
Feel the sun (or rain)
And I'm done
Didn't win but feel I've won

Life advice from Lucas (aged 6)
Work hard

Women: My Search Engine Findings
I turned to Google's predictions for help with this poem.
Results below:

why are girls so sensitive?
why are girls so cute?
why are girls called birds?
(do they like to hoot?)
why are girls more flexible?
why are girls so insecure?
why are girls shorter than boys?
(I'm actually not too sure. Probably hormone differences).

why are women colder than men?
why are women paid less?
why are women not funny?
(you can't be funny in a dress).
why are women so beautiful?
why are women attracted to men?
why are women so controlling?
(don't you dare say that again).

why are men taller than women?
why are men attracted to feet?
why are men and women so different?
(probably because of the toilet seat?)
why are men stronger than women?
why are menstrual cramps worse at night?
why are menthol cigarettes banned?
I'll stop Googling now. Good night.

Life advice from Emma Wilkinson
Rome wasn't built in a day

The Last Day

On the very last day
of course, we would play
like children
dancing
drawing shapes with our bodies
pressing crayons into paper
laughing at scribbles

If it was the end
of course, we would send
that letter
to that loved one
that friend

On the very last day
of course, we would say
let's meet now
let's show up for sunrise.

Life advice from Matt
Make every day count

ACKNOWLEDGEMENTS

To the 70 strangers that I spoke to: thank you. Not one person rejected my request for life advice. Yes, many were confused. Yes, some felt uncomfortable being put on the spot, but I would like to thank you all for your kindness in speaking with me. Each and every dialogue was incredibly unique and special.

Now I know it's not the Oscars but I'd like to, of course, thank my Mum, Dad and loving friends. Book, or no book, your ongoing support means the world to me.

I'd like to thank Fisher King Publishing. Thank you to Rick and the team for rolling with my crazy idea.

I also owe a huge thank you to Harry Whittaker and the team at BBC Radio York. Their ongoing support for the last two years really does make me speechless (not ideal for radio). It has been such an honor to be appointed their 'BBC Radio York Poet Laureate' and appear on the show every Saturday at 1.15pm to share a new poem.

I'd also like to thank Mrs Coull – my English teacher when I was at school. It means a lot when a teacher truly believes in you (it did to me anyway). She told me on multiple occasions that I '*was* a writer' and made me promise to 'keep writing.' Inspired by Mrs Coull's teaching style, I really focus on using positive encouragement around creativity when delivering my poetry workshops in schools.

Finally, a huge thank you to James, my loving partner and

number one supporter. When we first met and I told him I liked poetry he screwed up his nose in confusion and then politely said, "Oh. That's different." I swiftly moved conversation back to our shared passion for the outdoors. Four years later and differences aside, James always has and always will encourage me to follow my poetry dreams. He is my rock and I wouldn't have been able to complete this journey without him.

ABOUT THE AUTHOR

Liv's first book of poetry, Poems On The Gate Post, was published in 2020. Since then, she has made sharing her poetry with others top of her to do list. Liv has taken to the stage performing her poetry, she runs regular poetry workshops for both children and adults and at the start of 2021, was appointed BBC Radio York's Poet Laureate.

Facebook: Olivia Mulligan Poetry
Instagram: Liv_Mulligan_Poet

Lightning Source UK Ltd.
Milton Keynes UK
UKHW021236180821
389007UK00009B/90

9 781914 560033